WILLIAM H. HARRISON

PRESIDENTIAL ✦ LEADERS

WILLIAM H. HARRISON

MEG GREENE

TWENTY-FIRST CENTURY BOOKS/MINNEAPOLIS

For my father

Twenty-First Century Books
A division of Lerner Publishing Group
241 First Avenue North
Minneapolis, MN 55401 U.S.A.

Website address: www.lernerbooks.com

Library of Congress Cataloging-in-Publication Data

Greene, Meg.
    William H. Harrison / by Meg Greene.
       p.   cm. — (Presidential leaders)
    Includes bibliographical references and index.
    ISBN-13: 978-0-8225-1511-1 (lib. bdg. : alk. paper)
    ISBN-10: 0-8225-1511-3 (lib. bdg. : alk. paper)
    1. Harrison, William Henry, 1773-1841—Juvenile literature. 2. Presidents—United
States—Biography—Juvenile literature. I. Title.
    E392.G84 2007
    973.8'6092—dc22 [B]   2006021853

Manufactured in the United States of America
1 2 3 4 5 6 – JR – 12 11 10 09 08 07

CONTENTS

❖

William Henry Harrison

INTRODUCTION

Times change, and we change with them.
—William H. Harrison

The early morning hours of November 7, 1811, began with a cold, drizzly rain at the Tippecanoe River near present-day Lafayette, Indiana. Only the campfires offered relief from the bone-chilling cold. The clouds sometimes parted just enough to let the fading moonlight shine through. In the darkness, U.S. soldiers lay sleeping. They kept their guns by their sides in case of an attack. The soldiers, under the command of Governor William Henry Harrison, had come to the area to stop the growing threat from the Shawnees and other Native Americans.

Aware that his enemies were both brave and shrewd, Harrison took no chances with his troops—300 regular army troops and 650 men from local militias (small armies). He organized the fighters in a four-sided pattern. Around four o'clock in the morning, a number of Indians made their way silently toward the camp. War cries and gunfire shattered the peaceful quiet. Many of

Harrison's men awoke to find the Indians upon them. It was a total surprise.

When the attack at Tippecanoe began, Harrison emerged from his tent and grabbed what he thought was his gray mare. But instead, he mounted a different horse. The attackers concentrated their fire on the horse Harrison usually rode. The rider fell dead. The Indians thought they had killed Harrison, but they had actually shot his aide.

For the next two hours, Harrison's troops battled the determined Shawnees. Amid the swirling smoke and the thunder of gunfire, Harrison fought alongside his men. The Indians retreated when they ran out of ammunition. Hundreds of soldiers were killed or hurt. Even as his own soldiers pointed out his mistakes in the operation, Harrison sent a rider to Washington, D.C., to proclaim victory. This marked the beginning of a legend: the hero of Tippecanoe.

THE HERO OF TIPPECANOE

At the age of thirty-eight, William Henry Harrison had already experienced more of life than most people his age had. Born into one of the most important families in Virginia, Harrison was raised on a large, well-known plantation. His grandfather and father had served their country through politics.

Harrison's father hoped his son would become a doctor, but the young man chose a very different path. Stirred by thrilling stories he had heard about the western frontier, Harrison decided to become a soldier. By the time he was eighteen years old, he had landed an infantry post in the

Northwest Territory (modern Ohio, Indiana, Illinois, Michigan, and Wisconsin). In the 1790s, this area was at the far western edge of the new nation of the United States of America.

For the next twenty years, Harrison served with distinction in the U.S. Army. After leaving the service in 1798, Harrison entered politics, serving first as secretary of the Northwest Territory and later as the territorial governor.

In 1811 Harrison found himself back in uniform as tensions mounted with many Native American groups living in the Northwest Territory. After discussions failed to resolve the conflict, Harrison led his troops in the battle at Tippecanoe.

Although opinions differed about Harrison's performance at Tippecanoe, the battle made him famous. Years later, that fame played a key role in Harrison's quest to become a member of the House of Representatives, a senator, a diplomat and, finally, president of the United States.

CHAPTER ONE

CHILD OF THE REVOLUTION

*The days of his boyhood were the
epic days of American history.*

—James A. Green, Harrison biographer

William Henry Harrison grew up as a child of the
American Revolution (1775–1783). His family held deep
roots in the American colonies. As the son of a leading
Virginia statesman, William grew up listening to discussions
about the colonies' desire for independence from Great
Britain. William and his family experienced the
Revolutionary War firsthand, and he matured as the new
nation struggled to establish itself.

ROOTED IN HISTORY

Harrison was born in Charles City County, Virginia, on
February 9, 1773. At the time, Virginia was a colony of Great
Britain. William's ancestors were among the first English set-
tlers in Virginia. They had distinguished themselves in politics

William's father,
Benjamin Harrison V,
was a leading Virginia
statesman.

✧ ————————————

and public office, becoming one of the most important families in colonial Virginia.

William's father, Benjamin Harrison V, continued the
family tradition of holding political office. He served as a
representative to the House of Burgesses, Virginia's legislature. He had married Elizabeth Bassett, the daughter of a
plantation owner from New Kent County, Virginia.
William was the couple's seventh child. He had four older
sisters and two older brothers.

The family lived in a three-story brick home known as
Berkeley Plantation. Built in 1726 by William's grandfather, Benjamin Harrison IV, the home stood majestically
near the banks of the James River. The Harrisons owned

A Historic Home

Berkeley is one of the most famous plantation homes in Virginia. On December 4, 1619, pilgrims from England came ashore at what became Berkeley Plantation and observed the first Thanksgiving in America. After receiving a grant of twenty-two thousand acres of land, Benjamin Harrison IV (William Henry Harrison's grandfather) built the stately brick home on the plantation in 1726. Though not as large by the time of William's birth in 1773, Berkeley Plantation still included thousands of acres.

Besides tobacco fields, Berkeley also had a flour mill and a shipyard. In the fall, ships loaded with tobacco set sail from Harrison's Landing to Great Britain. The following spring or summer, the ships returned, bringing wine, furniture, books, and other goods for Harrison and his business partners.

Berkeley remained in the Harrison family until the Civil War (1861–1865). In 1862 the home served as headquarters for Union general George McClellan and 140,000 federal troops. President Abraham Lincoln visited the plantation twice that year to meet with McClellan. The Harrison family could not get Berkeley Plantation back after the war, and the house and grounds fell into ruin.

In 1907 John Jamieson, who had served as a drummer during the Civil War and had camped at Berkeley with Union

thousands of acres of farmland. They also kept more than one hundred slaves.

During his years in office, Benjamin Harrison became an outspoken critic of British colonial policy. He especially disliked the heavy taxes Britain imposed on the colonies. In 1773 Harrison joined the Virginia Committee of Correspondence.

William grew up at Berkeley Plantation in Virginia.
His father was a farmer and slave owner.

forces, bought the property. Jamieson's son Malcolm, who inherited the home in 1927, restored it to its original beauty. Berkeley is not only a popular tourist attraction but also remains a working farm.

Most of the American colonies had established such committees to oppose the British government. Committee members helped coordinate activities among the colonies as they pondered independence from Great Britain.

William spent his early childhood years against the backdrop of the American fight for independence.

In 1774, when William was barely one year old, his father was elected a delegate to the newly organized Continental Congress. This group of colonists met to discuss their common grievances, or complaints, against the British government. As the Congress prepared to meet in Philadelphia, William's father moved his family there. Benjamin Harrison presided over the debates that led to the composition of the Declaration of Independence. He was one of those who signed the Declaration in 1776.

———————————— ✧ ————————————

William's father, Benjamin (front, far left), was one of five Virginians who signed the Declaration of Independence.

REVOLUTION AND FREEDOM

The American Revolution was a war between Great Britain and thirteen British colonies in North America. The conflict began as a colonial revolt against British economic policies, such as high taxes on tea and other goods. Throughout the war, the British used their superior naval power to capture colonial coastal cities. But the colonists received money, soldiers, and equipment from other European powers, such as France and Spain. In 1781, at the Battle of Yorktown, the British army surrendered. The Treaty of Paris in 1783 recognized the independence of the newly formed United States of America.

British troops under the command of General Charles Cornwallis surrendered at Yorktown, Virginia, in 1781, ending the Revolutionary War.

A GRIM REMINDER OF WAR

By 1780 Benjamin Harrison and his family had moved back to Berkeley. Seven-year-old William felt like he was visiting for the first time, since he had been so young when the family moved to Philadelphia. William helped around the house and explored the plantation grounds. In the evenings, he listened to the many visitors who came by to talk with his father about the American fight for independence.

The Harrisons soon found the Revolutionary War at their doorstep. They learned that the British fleet had anchored nearby in Chesapeake Bay. A group of Hessians—German soldiers fighting for the British—and American Loyalists (colonists who sided with the British) arrived at Westover, a plantation just a few miles from Berkeley. William's father wasted little time getting his family to safety. He sent them to a relative's plantation. In the meantime, the soldiers moved on to Richmond, the new capital of Virginia. They plundered warehouses in search of food, weapons, ammunition, and other supplies.

But the Harrison family home was not out of danger. Returning from Richmond, the Hessians and the Loyalists, under the command of Benedict Arnold, who had once fought on the Americans' side, stopped at Berkeley. Arnold's men wreaked havoc on the abandoned plantation. They burned paintings, clothing, and furniture. The Harrisons' once-grand house stood nearly in ruins, its walls stripped bare and its rooms emptied. Fires smoldered everywhere. The troops also slaughtered cattle and other livestock and seized forty slaves and all the horses. They broke and toppled tombstones in the family graveyard.

The intrusion made a powerful impression on William. He began to understand the destruction of war. It took almost four years for the Harrisons to restore their home. The family finally returned to Berkeley in 1784.

GROWING UP AT BERKELEY

Even though William grew up during a tumultuous time, in many ways his childhood was unremarkable. A spirited and energetic boy, he roamed the grounds of Berkeley on foot and horseback. The nearby James River provided plenty of opportunities for fishing and swimming. Although he was physically small, William enjoyed the same activities as other boys his age.

Because no schools were nearby, William and his sisters and brothers attended school on the plantation. Every morning the children walked to a small brick building where a private tutor taught them to read and write. They also studied Latin and ancient history.

When not playing or studying, William loved to listen to his father talk with neighbors, friends, and relatives about affairs of the day. Years later, William entertained people with tales about the famous revolutionary leaders who visited Berkeley, including Patrick Henry, the Marquis de Lafayette, and George Washington. Young William listened attentively as the adults spoke of the war and the business of creating a new nation. As thrilling as those discussions were, his father's descriptions of the western frontier excited him even more. He enjoyed hearing about the vital role the West would play in the new country's future.

COLLEGE-BOUND

By the time William was fourteen, his father had concluded that William was not suited for a career in law or politics. Benjamin decided that his son should become a doctor instead. To prepare him for his future occupation, he sent William to Hampden-Sydney College, near the Blue Ridge Mountains west of Richmond. In the fall of 1787, William said his farewells to his family and boarded a stagecoach for the two-day journey to Prince Edward County.

At Hampden-Sydney, William studied Greek and Latin, history, geography, mathematics, and rhetoric (the art of speaking and writing persuasively). He enjoyed school. His favorite subjects included military history and Latin. Though he was a diligent student, William found time for

William attended Hampden-Sydney College (above) *for one year.*

———————————— ✧ ————————————

extracurricular activities. He helped to organize the campus literary society and participated in the Union Society, the college debate club.

After a year, however, William left the school and transferred to a small academy in Southampton County. In 1790 William's father sent him to Richmond to study with Dr. Andrew Leiper. While in Richmond, William began attending meetings of the Humane Society. The society was one of the first abolitionist, or antislavery, groups in the country.

William sympathized with their cause, even though his father owned a large number of slaves.

A NEW PATH

Still determined that his son would become a doctor, Benjamin Harrison enrolled William in the Medical School of Pennsylvania—the only medical school in the country at the time. Benjamin hoped that Dr. Benjamin Rush, a well-known doctor on the faculty, would take William under his wing. Benjamin had met Dr. Rush during the Revolution. The two had become good friends. In 1791 William boarded a ship bound for Philadelphia.

Terrible news awaited William when he arrived. His father had died on April 25, while William was on his way to Philadelphia. One of his father's last requests was that William remain in Philadelphia to continue his studies.

✧ ————————————

Benjamin Rush (left) was a prominent physician as well as a politician. Like Harrison's father, Rush had signed the Declaration of Independence.

A COLONIAL DOCTOR

Training to become a doctor during the colonial period did not involve the rigorous course of study that medical schools later required. Students at the medical school in Philadelphia attended two series of lectures for sixteen weeks each. But few students finished the course. Many left and served apprenticeships with practicing doctors, much as William did with Dr. Leiper in Richmond. Apprentices learned by watching and assisting the doctor.

William attended lectures in anatomy at Surgeons' Hall (below). The Medical School of Pennsylvania was the only medical school in the United States. Most doctors learned their skills as apprentices.

William dutifully began attending classes at Surgeons' Hall. But his heart was not in his work. He admired Dr. Rush but realized that a career in medicine was not for him.

William wanted to serve his country in some way. He sought a job in the federal government, but he had little success. Then, in August 1791, William met with one of his father's old friends, Richard Henry Lee, who was visiting Philadelphia. Lee suggested that if William really wanted to serve his country, he should join the military. Lee promised to arrange a commission (army post) for William directly from President Washington, another Harrison family friend.

————————————— ✧
Richard Henry Lee (right), *another signer of the Declaration of Independence, arranged for Harrison to receive his first commission.*

William quickly received an army post. He later wrote, "In 24 hours from the first [moment I had] the idea of changing my profession, I was an Ensign in the 1st U.S. [regiment] of Infantry."

In the fall of 1791, eighteen-year-old William Henry Harrison, along with eighty other recruits, left Philadelphia for the West. Many Native American groups lived in the area. At the same time, settlers from the new United States were pushing westward. The U.S. government set up forts as staging grounds for further expansion. As a result, the Indians saw the white army as intruders.

For Harrison's service in the U.S. Army, 1st U.S. Infantry, he would earn $2.10 (about $30 in modern money) a month. But neither his rank nor his pay mattered to him. What he looked forward to was a great adventure in the western wilds.

CHAPTER TWO

FIGHTING ON THE FRONTIER

*Mr. Harrison [is] one of the . . . most
promising Young Gentlemen in the Army.*
—General James Wilkinson, 1792

After marching for three weeks and three hundred miles, his feet swollen and calloused, William Henry Harrison at last arrived with his company at Fort Pitt. The fort, near the future site of Pittsburgh, Pennsylvania, marked the edge of the Northwest Territory and the western frontier. (The Northwest Territory spanned about 260,000 square miles in the states near the Great Lakes.) The crude wooden fort stood between the Allegheny and the Monongahela rivers, which joined to form the Ohio River.

Harrison arrived in mid-October 1791. The overland trip had been hard. Much of the land was rough and mountainous. The food was terrible, and the days were long. Yet Harrison's sense of adventure had not faded. He was excited to be walking the land that his father and others had only talked about. He carried little from home except two dog-eared texts: a book of rhetoric and a book in Latin by Cicero, an ancient Roman statesman and author. When not marching, drilling, or attending to his military duties, Harrison made the most of every spare minute by reading.

ON TO FORT WASHINGTON

Soon after arriving at Fort Pitt, Harrison and the other soldiers prepared to move on to Fort Washington, located on the Ohio River near present-day Cincinnati, Ohio. Military scouts had sighted Indians in the area. The fort needed

Harrison traveled more than four hundred miles along the Ohio River from Fort Pitt in Pennsylvania to Fort Washington (above) in the Northwest Territory.

more troop support. The soldiers in Harrison's company gathered timber to build flatboats, which would carry them up the river to Fort Washington.

Although the boats provided a welcome relief from the tiresome days of marching, Harrison and the others had to be careful. The river was full of potential dangers: jagged rocks that could break apart a flatboat and low tree limbs that could sweep a man overboard. The soldiers kept talk to a minimum for fear of attracting the attention of Indians. At night, under the cover of darkness, the men drifted along quietly. They rarely stopped to camp onshore. The sight of a fire, the smell of smoke, or the sound of talk and laughter might alert the Indians that their enemy was close by. Harrison encountered no Indians on the journey, however. It was as if the frontier was completely deserted except for the birds and animals he saw. Harrison was more concerned about what he could not see.

A Soldier's Life

Few men volunteered to serve in the army during the eighteenth century. The pay was low. The food was bad. The assignments were dangerous. The equipment was scarce and often in poor condition. Training for the new recruits was haphazard at best. Yet the U.S. military desperately needed soldiers, so recruiters turned away very few who wished to enlist. To entice men to join, recruiting officers often staged small parades with drummers, fifers (flute players), and perhaps a soldier or two.

Harrison and his company traveled along the Ohio River to Fort Washington on a flatboat like the one above. Flatboats were oblong boxes made to carry large loads. Boaters guided the flatboats with large oars.

——————————— ✧ ———————————

Native Americans living in the Northwest Territory posed a serious threat. The Shawnee, Delaware, Miami, Sauk, Kickapoo, and Potawatomi had cause to dislike white people, particularly the Americans. While the English and the French had tried to maintain fairly good relations with the Indians, the Americans had continually tried to take over Indian land. The building of new forts signaled to the Indians that the Americans intended not only to stay but also to bring even more settlers into the area.

After the Revolution, the Shawnee, who had sided with the British during the war, continued to fight the Americans. Shawnee leaders hoped to stop the Americans from moving onto Indian lands. Fort Washington was a major target, and tensions inside the fort were high. To meet the Shawnee threat, the commander of the post, General Arthur St. Clair, set out from Fort Washington with several thousand men. St. Clair hoped to surprise the Shawnee and defeat them before they had a chance to strike. Tecumseh, a Shawnee warrior who

General Arthur St. Clair

———— ✧ ————

had led a scouting party to spy on the Americans, reported St. Clair's movement to the Shawnee chiefs. They prepared for battle. Although U.S. forces far outnumbered the Indians, the Americans were struggling. The soldiers lacked discipline and were ill equipped for frontier warfare.

ST. CLAIR'S DEFEAT

On November 4, 1791, in the hours just before daybreak, Tecumseh and his warriors attacked St. Clair's men. The surprised Americans never recovered. Many soldiers threw down their guns and fled. Others fought, but their efforts came to nothing. The Shawnee killed more than six hundred U.S. soldiers and the fifty-six women who traveled with the troops to cook and do laundry.

TECUMSEH

For thirty years after the American Revolution, the great Native American leader Tecumseh fought to keep U.S. settlers out of the Ohio River valley. Born in 1768 in western Ohio, Tecumseh became an orphan at the age of six when settlers killed his father, who was an important Shawnee chief. An older sister and brother raised Tecumseh, and the Shawnee chief Blackfish adopted him. From an early age, Tecumseh hated the American settlers who were taking Shawnee lands and lives.

By the time of the American Revolution, Tecumseh had begun working to protect his people. Traveling throughout the Great Lakes region, Tecumseh urged unity among tribes: "Brothers we must be united; we must smoke the same pipe; we must fight each other's battles; and more than all, we must love the Great Spirit. He is for us. He will destroy our enemies and make all his red children happy."

Tecumseh

Tecumseh was a powerful speaker, skilled warrior, and respected leader. He soon rallied many other tribes to his cause.

Few of St. Clair's troops escaped to tell of the terrible defeat the army had suffered.

Unaware of what had taken place, Harrison and the others arrived at Fort Washington. They were startled by the sight of men and women abandoning the fort. The survivors wore little more than rags and had few supplies. St. Clair's defeat taught Harrison a valuable lesson. When he heard that many of St. Clair's soldiers were untrained militia, Harrison vowed never to allow a soldier under his command to fight until he had been properly trained.

Harrison and others in his regiment occupied the fort and tried to restore order. Because Harrison had received his army commission through political influence rather than active service, he found himself the target of resentment from others in his unit. Many of these soldiers and officers were veterans of the Revolutionary War and thought Harrison was too young and inexperienced. One officer even encouraged him to resign. But Harrison refused and went about his duties.

In the early months of 1792, General St. Clair gave Harrison his first command. Harrison was to lead a small detail of twenty men and packhorses to bring supplies to Fort Hamilton, a new fort twenty-five miles north of Fort Washington. Other soldiers waited to see how Harrison would handle himself.

Although Harrison and his men endured bitterly cold weather, the journey to Fort Hamilton proved uneventful. They reached the new fort and returned safely to Fort Washington. St. Clair was so pleased with Harrison that he rewarded him with public praise. Harrison made two more journeys for St. Clair in the winter of 1792–1793.

Fort Hamilton (above) was the first U.S. Army fort built north of Fort Washington in Native American lands.

─────────────── ✧ ───────────────

A BOOST IN RANK

By 1793 twenty-year-old Harrison had been in the army for more than two years. He had distinguished himself as a capable and respected soldier. Harrison had grown fond of army life and liked the frontier. He returned to Virginia only once, to attend his mother's funeral. While at Berkeley, he sold the land he had inherited to his older brother. In exchange, Harrison received money and another piece of land in Kentucky. Harrison considered the West his home.

During Harrison's time in the army, the military made some dramatic changes. St. Clair's defeat had prompted the U.S. Congress to give the military more money for troops, better training, and equipment. Harrison also had a new commanding officer, General Anthony Wayne. Wayne was

General Anthony Wayne (right) mentored young Harrison in the art and skills of warfare.

——————————— ✧

considered one of the best American generals in the Revolutionary War. A masterful commander, he won many victories and earned the nickname Mad Anthony for his seemingly crazy military feats. In 1792 Congress had promoted him to major general and sent him westward to fight the Indians in the Ohio Valley.

Under Wayne's watchful eye, Harrison learned a great deal about frontier combat. Harrison, in turn, impressed the general with his careful attention to duty. Wayne promoted Harrison to lieutenant and made him his aide-de-camp (a commanding officer's chief assistant). Along with his new rank and duties, Harrison received a raise in pay to $64 (about $900) a month, an increase in his daily food ration, and an additional $12 ($170) a month to pay for feed for his horses.

In the early summer of 1793, General Wayne waited anxiously for some important news. Three U.S. commissioners were meeting with representatives from several tribes in the Northwest Territory, hoping to reach a peace settlement. The discussions did not go well. But the Indians agreed that if the Americans advanced no farther than the Ohio River, the tribes would end hostilities. The Americans refused.

By fall, war with the Indians seemed near. But the winter passed quietly. In February 1794, Harrison received orders to escort a group of Native American leaders who wished to meet with General Wayne. The leaders com-

────────────── ✧ ──────────────

The Northwest Territory was a violent and scary place in the late 1700s. Still, many settlers moved there so they could own their own land.

plained to Wayne about the army's preparations for war and requested a truce. Wayne offered a truce on the condition that the Indians surrender all white prisoners. This time the Indians refused.

The time for talk had passed. In June 1794, Indian warriors attacked Fort Recovery, which the Americans had built near the site of St. Clair's defeat. The nation was at war once again. The Indians received support from the British, who also hoped to defeat the Americans. British soldiers arrived to join the Indians' fight.

FALLEN TIMBERS

On July 28, 1794, General Wayne left the winter quarters he had established at Fort Greenville, Ohio. Leading an army of three thousand men, he made his way to Fort Miami, which the British had constructed along the Maumee River (near present-day Toledo, Ohio). The journey was long and difficult under the scorching summer sun. During the day, the soldiers marched in long columns to prevent ambush. Each night, Wayne ordered them to chop down trees to build walls to protect themselves.

Indian scouts marked the progress of Wayne's army. Tecumseh realized that the Americans were a formidable enemy. It was unlikely that they would allow themselves to be surprised. Meanwhile, Wayne's scouts reported that a large number of Indian warriors were gathering near the fort.

On August 20, 1794, Wayne and his army were less than five miles from Fort Miami. Wayne ordered his men to drop their packs and march in complete silence. Riding next to Wayne, Harrison relayed orders between Wayne and the junior officers. Harrison could not conceal his growing excitement. The coming fight would be his first experience in battle. Harrison had another reason to be excited. General Wayne had decided to follow Harrison's earlier suggestion to advance in two columns and have the soldiers drop their packs so that they could move more quickly. Harrison also recommended—and Wayne agreed—that the men at the center of the columns carry the artillery and spare ammunition.

When Wayne's men were within three miles of the fort, they came upon hundreds of trees that had fallen in a terrible storm. The trees provided cover for the four hundred

Wayne's troops fight Tecumseh's army in the battle at Fallen Timbers.

Indian warriors and one hundred British soldiers who lay in wait for the Americans. The trees also gave the battle its name: Fallen Timbers.

When the British and the Indians opened fire, the first line of U.S. cavalry scattered in confusion. Wayne ordered his men to charge the enemy, and he sent Harrison to restore order to the troops. Harrison succeeded, and soon the Americans were attacking the Indians and the British from two sides. Harrison rode back and forth, conveying Wayne's orders and informing him about the progress of

————————— ✧
After suffering grave losses in the battle at Fallen Timbers, British and Indian fighters retreated.

the battle. The Americans pressed forward. The Indians and the British retreated, carrying their dead and wounded to the shelter of Fort Miami. Once the British soldiers were safely inside, however, they closed the gate and refused to allow the Indians to enter. Tecumseh never forgot or forgave this act of British treachery.

As quickly as it had started, the battle at Fallen Timbers was finished. The Indians fled. The next day, Wayne decided not to attack the fort. As the Americans retreated, however, they burned Indian villages and crops, British trading houses, and the home of one British officer.

On November 2, the weary Americans reached their camp at Fort Greenville. In his official report, Wayne singled out several officers who had shown great courage in battle. One was Lieutenant William Henry Harrison. Wayne wrote that he "did all the riding to give orders from the commander-in-chief. And where the [hottest] of the action raged there we could see Harrison give the order. It's my . . . opinion, if he continues a military man, he will be a second Washington." At just twenty-one years old, William Henry Harrison was beginning to make his mark in service to his country.

Harrison in his army uniform in the early 1800s

CHAPTER THREE

WADING THE POLITICAL WATERS

*Mr. Harrison . . . Father of the Land System
and the Poor Man's Friend*
—Charles Stewart Todd and Benjamin Drake, 1840

Victory in the battle at Fallen Timbers temporarily ended hostilities in the Ohio Valley. On August 3, 1795, U.S. officials met with a number of tribal chiefs to sign the Treaty of Greenville. Under the terms of the treaty, the Indians gave up lands that later became the state of Ohio and parts of Indiana, Michigan, and Illinois. Tecumseh, however, scorned the chiefs' attempts to make peace and rejected the treaty. He began crisscrossing the vast territory of the Ohio Valley, seeking to unite the tribes to resist white settlement.

In the fall of 1795, Harrison was serving as assistant quartermaster at Fort Washington. The job was very important. As quartermaster, Harrison secured food, clothing, horses, feed for the horses, and other goods the army needed.

By now a seasoned veteran of the frontier, Harrison had gained a reputation as a fearless soldier. At the age of twenty-two, Harrison was slim and of average height. He had a thin face with a sharp-bridged nose, close-set eyes, thin lips, and a strong jaw. His brown hair fell carelessly to one side of his face. He had an easy manner and a quick wit. Never one to waste time, Harrison kept up his habit of reading when not on duty. He especially enjoyed the Bible and books about military science. He also enjoyed horseback riding and taking brisk morning walks. Although he could have boasted about his accomplishments in battle, Harrison remained modest. Many other soldiers sought his companionship.

MEETING MISS ANNA

That fall Harrison enjoyed the companionship of more than just his fellow soldiers. He was secretly involved with a "remarkably beautiful girl" he had met earlier in the year on a trip to Lexington, Kentucky, for military business. Anna Tuthill Symmes was the daughter of John Cleves Symmes, a former member of Congress and a noted judge. Judge Symmes owned about one million acres of land, making him one of the wealthiest landowners in the Northwest Territory.

Harrison and Anna were immediately attracted to each other and soon fell in love. Judge Symmes was not happy with the relationship, however. He liked Harrison and thought he was of good character. But he did not want his daughter to marry a soldier. When Harrison requested

As a young woman, Anna Tuthill Symmes (seen here in her later years) fell quickly in love with Harrison.
—————— ✧

Anna's hand in marriage, Judge Symmes refused to give his consent. The judge explained that he did not believe Harrison could support a wife and family on his meager pay as an army lieutenant. The judge ordered Harrison to stop seeing his daughter.

Harrison and Anna disobeyed her father's command and continued to meet secretly. On November 25, 1795, while Judge Symmes was away on business, Harrison and Anna married at the home of a local doctor. The couple rode fourteen miles to Fort Washington, where they planned to live. For two weeks, Harrison did not see his father-in-law. When they finally met at a dinner party, the judge asked Harrison how he would support Anna. Harrison replied:

John Cleves Symmes was slow to approve of his daughter's marriage to a soldier.

✧ ———————————

"My sword is my means of support sir!" In time, Judge Symmes accepted his daughter's marriage and his new son-in-law. He acknowledged that Harrison's "best prospect is the army[;] he has talents." The judge believed that if Harrison could stay out of the way of the bullets, he would make a name for himself as a military hero.

The following year, the Harrisons had another reason to celebrate. They welcomed their first child, Elizabeth Bassett, known as Betsy.

A NEW DIRECTION

In the spring of 1798, President John Adams appointed Harrison secretary of the Northwest Territory, a post that paid $1,200 (about $17,000) a year. Meanwhile, Harrison

President John Adams appointed Harrison secretary of the Northwest Territory in 1798.

——————— ✧

had reached the rank of captain. Colonel Winthrop Sargent had recommended Harrison for the position, writing, "Captain Harrison [is] a Young Gentleman of Virginia, and of Education . . . who for seven years . . . has sustained a fair, indeed unblemished reputation as a Military officer. . . . I may venture to Vouch that he will not betray any trust, with which [the] Government may honour him—Indeed I think him a very deserving young man." With this appointment, Harrison made the difficult decision to resign from the military. Along with his new job, Harrison had a new baby. The Harrisons named their second child John Cleves Symmes.

As territorial secretary, Harrison had plenty to do. By the late 1790s, so many people had settled in the Northwest Territory that it had a House of Representatives, a governing

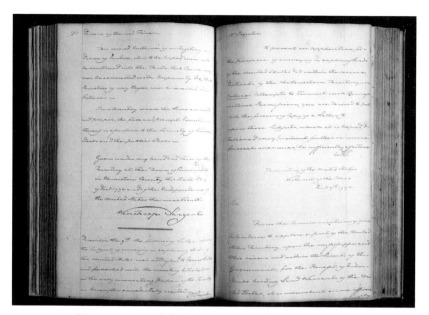

Harrison recorded official territorial business in the
Executive Journal of the Northwest Territory (above).

————————— ✧ —————————

council, and a representative in the U.S. Congress. One of
Harrison's duties was to record the activities of the territorial
government. At first Harrison welcomed the change from his
military duties. Soon, however, he grew bored with the rou-
tine. He set his eyes on a grander prize: the territorial delegate's seat in the U.S. Congress.

Harrison's decision to enter politics came at a very
important moment in the history of the Northwest
Territory. To make it easier for settlers to buy land, the federal government sold plots in the territory at cheap prices.
But the laws governing the sale of land favored speculators—buyers who did not farm the land but instead resold
it for a profit. Speculators purchased huge tracts from the

federal government for about $2 ($28) an acre. They then divided the tracts into smaller sections, selling them to set-tlers for a much higher price. Harrison, who himself had purchased land for about $3 ($43) an acre, wanted to change the laws so that people without much money could buy land cheaply, as the government intended.

In the nation's early years, political parties were still evolving. By the 1790s, two national political parties had emerged: the Democratic-Republicans, or Jeffersonians, and the Federalists. The Democratic-Republicans tended to draw support from small merchants and small farmers. They believed that the states should have more power than the U.S. government. In contrast, the Federalists supported business interests and favored a strong, centralized U.S. gov-ernment. Their main support came from wealthy business-people and landowners in the Northeast.

Harrison joined the Democratic-Republican Party. He met with several Democratic-Republican leaders and told them that he was interested in running for territorial dele-gate. If elected, he pledged to reform the land laws. That convinced party officials to support his candidacy.

DELEGATE TO CONGRESS

Harrison's opponent in the congressional race was Arthur St. Clair Jr. St. Clair was the son of the former commander of Fort Washington. A firm Federalist, St. Clair opposed any reform of the land laws. Harrison won the delegate's seat by a slender margin. In December 1799, he prepared to move to Philadelphia, then the home of the federal gov-ernment. People in Philadelphia were eager to get a look at Harrison. Because he had spent years on the frontier, they expected him to be rough and uneducated, dressed in buckskin, and toting a shotgun. Harrison surprised them. He was well educated and well spoken.

True to his word, Harrison presented a public land bill on February 18, 1800. Under his proposal, the government would sell plots of 320 acres to settlers for less than two dollars an acre. Those without enough money to buy a tract all at once could pay for part of it, with the promise to pay the rest in four years. Harrison hoped that his bill would limit land speculation and give many more people the opportunity to buy land in the Northwest Territory.

Federalists in Congress attacked Harrison's proposal. They argued that it was risky to allow people to buy land on credit, with no guarantee that they would pay back the money they owed in four years. Harrison responded that only the wealthy benefited from the current system. Harrison's argument struck a chord with many legislators. On April 2, 1800, the Harrison Land Act passed. It was an impressive political victory for Harrison.

Another piece of legislation that Harrison sponsored had an even greater effect on his political career. In the Northwest Territory, only three judges supervised all legal proceedings. Given the vast size of the region, the job was becoming too much for three men to handle. To make their job easier, Harrison suggested that the territory be divided into two parts. On March 31, 1800, after much debate, Congress approved the division of the Northwest Territory. The eastern region consisted of Ohio. The western region— to be called Indiana Territory—encompassed the future states of Indiana, Illinois, Michigan, and Wisconsin. The new territory's capital was Vincennes, Indiana.

All that remained was to find a suitable person to be the first governor for the new Indiana Territory. President Adams asked Harrison if he would take the job. At first Harrison hesitated. But with the birth of his third child, Lucy Singleton, he had to consider the needs of his growing family. Harrison decided to accept the commission. He was twenty-seven years old.

Settlers clear land and build a cabin. In the early 1800s, Indiana Territory was sparsely populated, but that soon changed.

CHAPTER FOUR

GOVERNOR OF THE FRONTIER

W. H. Harrison . . . is highly esteemed by all who know him. . . . His abilities . . . will be of infinite service to the western interest.
—Congressman C. S. Wau, 1802

Harrison arrived at Vincennes in early January 1801. A few days later, on January 10, he was sworn in as governor of the Indiana Territory. The inauguration took place in a small two-story building that served as the territorial capitol. Harrison then met with William Clark, the territory's chief justice, Secretary John Gibson, and two judges, Henry Vanderburgh and John Griffin. Together, these five men made up the territorial government.

In 1801 the Indiana Territory had a population of about twelve thousand Native Americans and six thousand white settlers. The whites lived mainly in the southern part of the territory. The capital, Vincennes, stood near the banks of

*Harrison and his administrators oversaw the Indiana Territory
from the capitol building (above) in Vincennes.*

———————————— ◇ ————————————

the Wabash River. Established in 1732, Vincennes—once
the site of a French fort and trading post—was the oldest
settlement in Indiana Territory. In 1801 Vincennes had
1,533 residents. Many were descendants of the original
French settlers.

The old French fort still stood near the riverbank. Just
beyond was a small church. The town also had a tavern,
where men met to drink, talk, and gamble. The streets were
unpaved. Residents lived in log cabins. From this frontier
settlement surrounded by forest and prairie, Governor
Harrison and his four administrators oversaw the territory.

The men dealt first with the most pressing business: orga-
nizing a court system to hear cases and forming a militia to

protect residents from Indians and other threats. By the middle of February, these tasks were done. Harrison returned to Kentucky, where his family was staying.

GROUSELAND

Harrison and his family made their way to Vincennes that April, arriving on May 15, 1801. The governor decided to build a new home, similar to Berkeley and the other elegant homes he had visited during his boyhood. He chose a site along the banks of the Wabash River near a grove of walnut trees. He named the home Grouseland, for the grouse (a type of game bird) that were so plentiful in the region.

Because skilled carpenters and masons (stone and brick workers) were hard to find in Indiana Territory, Harrison brought in workers from Pittsburgh. The home took several years to complete. In the meantime, the family stayed at a four-hundred-acre farm that Harrison had purchased. The farm included an orchard, a small dairy herd, and pigs. In this way, Harrison could provide food for his growing family and sell any surplus for profit.

Harrison looked for other ways to supplement his salary of $2,000 ($27,000) a year. He occasionally bought and sold real estate. At a new settlement near the Blue River, Harrison built sawmills to cut lumber and gristmills to grind grain. He also drew up plans to build a shipyard at Vincennes to help boost trade in goods from the area.

Occupied with his duties as governor, Harrison looked forward to the times when he could relax at home, hunt, or fish. He continued to enjoy taking long walks and riding horses. He was also devoted to his family. Harrison and his wife loved to entertain, and Grouseland became a center for

GROUSELAND

Built of brick and standing two stories high, Grouseland was the most magnificent home in Indiana Territory. It had thirteen rooms and four chimneys. Workers used walnut trees from the nearby woods to panel the house's walls. Harrison imported glass from Great Britain for the windows. The exterior walls were 18 inches thick. To beautify the grounds, his wife planted flower gardens and fruit trees.

Harrison took every precaution to keep his home and family safe from Indian attack. Heavy wooden shutters protected the six-foot-high windows. The attic windows had broad sills to provide sharpshooters a steady aim. Harrison also had workers build a room for storing gunpowder and a small lookout station on the roof. Harrison later added an underground tunnel so his family could escape if the house ever came under attack.

The cost of building Grouseland was quite high. To pay for the brick alone, Harrison bartered four hundred acres of land, with an estimated value of $1,000 ($14,000).

social gatherings. A charming host, Harrison amused guests with his humor and lively conversation. One visitor to Grouseland wrote, "Mr. H is a man of some merit, has handsome manners . . . in conversation is sprightly and gay."

Harrison loved his new home. "I am much pleased with this country," he declared. "Nothing can exceed its beauty and fertility."

During Harrison's time as governor of Indiana Territory, he and Anna hosted many parties at Grouseland (above).

TENDING TO BUSINESS

One of the most difficult challenges Harrison faced as governor was staying on good terms with Native Americans. Except for the land that the United States gained in the Treaty of Greenville, most of Indiana Territory was in the hands of various Indian nations, including the Miami, the Potawatomi, the Sauk, the Fox, the Kickapoo, and the Shawnee. Although the Indians held legal claim to the land, they could do little to stop white people from moving onto their territory.

Since many whites ignored the treaties and treated Native Americans with hostility, Harrison understood the Indians' anger. After meeting with representatives of various tribes, he wrote:

> *I believe that most [Native Americans] feel a friendship for the United States . . . but they make heavy complaints of ill-treatment. . . . They say their people have been killed, their lands settled on—their game . . . destroyed—& their young men made drunk & cheated. . . . Of the truth of these charges I am well convinced.*

Harrison did his best to keep the peace. He put in place a number of policies designed to help the Indians. He urged them to receive shots that would protect them from deadly illnesses such as smallpox. He issued orders forbidding whites from hunting and settling on Indian lands. He outlawed the sale of whiskey to Indians. Often when Indians brought valuable furs to trade, white traders took advantage of them by selling them cheap whiskey instead of food, clothing, or other necessities. As a result, many Indians became ill or died. Harrison withdrew the trading licenses of those who cheated or abused Indians. He also worked hard to bring to justice whites who murdered Indians. Despite his efforts, Harrison was only moderately successful.

Harrison was in a difficult position. Although he was trying to maintain peaceful relations with the Indians and protect their lands, he had to carry out the policies of

BY WILLIAM HENRY HARRISON,

GOVERNOR OF THE INDIANA TERRITORY, AND SUPERINTENDANT OF INDIAN AFFAIRS.

WHEREAS *Benoist Bizayou* . ——— of the county of *Knox* ——— ha th made application for permiſſion to trade with the *Miamies* nation of Indians, and ha th given bond according to law, for the due obſervance of all the laws and regulations for the government of the trade with Indians that now are, or hereafter may be enacted and eſta- bliſhed, licenſe is hereby granted to the ſaid *Benoist Bizayou* to trade with the ſaid *Miamies* nation, at their townſon the *Wabash* and thereto ſell, barter and exchange with the individuals of the ſaid nation, all manner of goods, wares and merchandizes, conformably to the laws and regulations aforeſaid ; but under this expreſs condition and reſtriction, that the ſaid *Benoist Bizayou* ſhall not, by *his* ——— ſervants, agents or factors, carry or cauſe to be carried to the hunting camps of the Indians of ſaid nation, any ſpecies of goods or merchandize whatſoever, and more eſpecially ſpirituous liquors of any kind ; nor ſhall barter or exchange the ſame, or any of them, in any quantity whatever, on pain of forfeiture of this licenſe, and of the goods, wares and merchandize, and of the ſpirituous liquors which may have been carried to the ſaid camps, contrary to the true intent and meaning hereof, and of having *his* bond put in ſuit: and the Indians of the ſaid nation are at full liberty to ſeize and confiſcate the ſaid liquors ſo carried, and the owner or owners ſhall have no claim for the ſame, either upon the ſaid nation, or any individual thereof, nor upon the United States.

This licenſe to continue in force for one year, unleſs ſooner revoked.

GIVEN under my hand and ſeal, the *Thirtieth* day of *December* , in the year of our Lord one thouſand eight hundred and *Seven* .

Willm Henry Harrison

As governor of Indiana Territory, Harrison issued licenses (above) to trade with the Indians. Harrison's signature and seal are at the bottom.

——————————— ✧ ———————————

President Thomas Jefferson. Jefferson insisted that the United States must extend its boundaries westward to the Mississippi River. This goal required the government to relocate many Indian tribes. Harrison was expected to negotiate with them to give up their ancestral homelands to the United States.

Harrison tried to convince the Indian leaders that if their people learned to farm, they would not need such large tracts of land for hunting and fishing. He assured them that the government would help them build farms and would teach them how to grow crops and raise live-stock. But both Harrison and the chiefs realized that, one way or another, the U.S. government would force the Indians to give up their lands and move westward. During his years as governor, Harrison negotiated several land treaties with the Indians. He acquired nearly all the land that makes up the states of Illinois and Indiana.

THE QUESTION OF SLAVERY

Another problem brewing during Harrison's administration was whether to permit slavery in the Indiana Territory. The Ordinance of 1787 banned slavery in the Northwest Territory. Residents who had already brought slaves into the territory were allowed to keep them. But as more Americans moved westward, many wanted to bring slaves with them.

When Harrison took office in 1801, about 135 slaves resided in Indiana Territory. Most lived in Vincennes or in the nearby settlements of Kaskaskia and Prairie du Roche. In the western part of the Northwest Territory, the descendants of French settlers and Americans from Virginia and Kentucky also held slaves. These slave owners wanted to build large plantations similar to those in the South. For this reason, slavery opponents referred to the slaveholders as "Virginia aristocrats."

When Harrison became governor of Indiana Territory, most white residents seemed to support slavery in the territory. In 1802 Harrison called a convention at Vincennes to ask the national government to allow slaves into Indiana Territory. Congress refused. In Harrison's personal life, the year brought some good news with the birth of his fourth child, William Henry Jr.

Since his request to repeal (strike down) the Ordinance of 1787 had failed, in 1803 Harrison proposed a territorial law to allow slavery. But a growing number of settlers in the Northwest Territory opposed slavery. They saw Harrison's attempt to get rid of the ordinance as an effort to aid slaveholders at the expense of the citizens who opposed slavery. Harrison had not realized how many people wanted to keep the ban on slavery.

Tied to the slavery question was the issue of statehood. By 1804 Indiana Territory had enough eligible voters to elect a congressional delegate. Both the proslavery and antislavery factions wanted a delegate who would represent their interests. Over the next several years, the territorial legislature argued about slavery. As Harrison tried to please both the proslavery and antislavery factions, Anna gave birth to three more children: John Scott in 1804, Benjamin in 1806, and Mary Symmes in 1809.

In 1809 Indiana's antislavery group finally gained the advantage, and the legislature presented a petition to Congress that forever banned slavery in the territory. For Harrison the measure was a serious defeat. He feared that it would destroy his chances of being reappointed. But in the middle of the tensions over slavery, another and potentially more dangerous threat captured Harrison's attention. Growing unrest among the Indians signaled the likely outbreak of war.

Harrison negotiated many treaties with the Indians in Indiana Territory.

CHAPTER FIVE

THE HERO OF TIPPECANOE

The clear, calm voice of General Harrison was heard in words of heroism in every part of the encampment during the action.

—Isaac Naylor, participant in the battle at Tippecanoe, 1811

Most of the treaties that Harrison negotiated worked against the Native Americans. They gave up millions of acres of their land in exchange for a little money and the promise of land farther west. Harrison once paid the Indians a penny for each two hundred acres in a deal that transferred fifty-one million acres to the United States. The Native Americans signed some treaties after losing battles. Other treaties stemmed from long negotiation.

Harrison also was acting superintendent of Indian Affairs for Indiana Territory. Although the federal government employed a small number of agents to work with the tribes, in the territories, there was no clear or focused

Indian policy. Territorial governors managed their dealings with the tribes as best they could.

A TALE OF TWO BROTHERS

The Shawnee chief Tecumseh continued to urge Native Americans to resist white settlement. He believed that if all the tribes joined together, they could prevent more whites from coming and perhaps drive out or kill those already there. Traveling throughout the Northwest Territory, Tecumseh met with various Native American leaders, hoping to persuade them to join his cause. Harrison realized that Tecumseh was a dangerous man. But he was not the only threat to Harrison's territory.

Tenskwatawa, also known as the Prophet, was Tecumseh's younger brother. Tenskwatawa preached a return to traditional

✧ ——————————
Tenskwatawa, Tecumseh's younger brother, had many followers.

In his preaching, Tenskwatawa urged Indians to oppose whites.

——————————— ✧

Indian ways. He called on the Indians to force white people off tribal homelands. According to Tenskwatawa, the Great Spirit had appeared to him in a vision, telling him that the Indians must abandon all white goods and customs. The Indians' growing reliance on guns, iron cookware, glass beads, alcohol, and other European items were terrible sins. If the people did not change their ways, Tenskwatawa said, the Great Spirit would not send the Indians to heaven. But if they did return to traditional ways, the Great Spirit would reward them by driving the white settlers away and allowing the Indians to go to heaven when they died.

The Prophet's message attracted many followers. But Tecumseh was a far more realistic and practical leader than his brother. He was not only a skilled warrior but also a masterful politician and diplomat. He understood that if the Indians did not work together, the whites would eventually overwhelm them. Tecumseh continued to build a political and military alliance among various tribes, while his brother reinforced the effort through his preaching.

By 1805 Harrison found himself almost entirely preoccupied with preventing war. It was no easy task. Nervous whites attacked and killed Indians, and Indians responded in kind. British government agents in the territory also spurred the Indians to violence. Bitter at having lost the war against the American colonies, the British encouraged

————————————— ✧ —————————————

Violence between white settlers and Indians
was common in the western territories.

the Indians to rise up against the United States. The British supplied the Indians with weapons and ammunition.

THE ECLIPSE

Harrison set out to weaken Tecumseh's influence among the Indian nations and to discredit the Prophet. In a letter to the Delaware people, Harrison warned that the Prophet "speaks not the words of the Great Spirit but those of the devil, and of the British agents." Like many other white men of the time, Harrison treated the Indians like children. He believed that they could not make good decisions on their own. He wrote, "My children, tread back the steps you have taken and endeavor to regain the straight road. Who is this pretended prophet who dares to speak in the name of the Great Creator?" he continued. "Demand of him some proofs. . . . If he is really a prophet, ask him to cause the sun to stand still or the moon to alter its course, the rivers to cease to flow, or the dead to rise from their graves."

Unfortunately, Harrison's message to the Delaware fell into the hands of a British agent, who passed it on to the Prophet. The Prophet gathered many of his followers and promised to ask the Great Spirit to blacken the sun. Earlier, a British agent may have told him that an eclipse would occur.

June 17, 1806, was a sunny day. Clothed in his flowing robes, the Prophet stood quietly. Just after eleven o'clock, he pointed to the sky and prayed to the Great Spirit to darken the sun. At that moment, the moon crossed in front of the sun and blotted it out. The sky darkened. Terrified, the crowd begged the Prophet to make the sun return. As the moon passed, the sun once again began to shine. The

Prophet's success won him greater fame and more supporters. When Harrison heard of the event, he realized that the
Prophet was not going to be easy to defeat.

RUMORS OF WAR

In 1808 the Prophet and Tecumseh set up a new headquarters where the Tippecanoe and Wabash rivers meet. Large
numbers of Tenskwatawa's followers moved to the village,
known as Prophetstown. In the meantime, Tecumseh
cemented the political and military alliance of the Indian
nations to drive whites out of Indiana Territory.

Rumors spread that the Indians at Prophetstown
planned to go to war. Harrison summoned two units of
the territorial militia, but when nothing happened, he
sent the troops home. During the summer of 1809, the
Prophet called on Harrison at Vincennes. During the
course of their discussions, Tenskwatawa claimed to want
peace and pledged his allegiance to the United States. But
Harrison suspected that the Prophet was deceiving him.
He believed that the Prophet still intended to fight and
that he and Tecumseh would get help from the British.

Early that September, Harrison met with representatives of a number of tribes. He hoped to buy about three
million acres along the Wabash and White rivers. In
exchange, according to the Treaty of Fort Wayne, the
Native Americans received goods valued at $1,500
($20,800) and an annual payment of $1,750 ($24,300)
to be divided among the tribes. Harrison regarded the
Treaty of Fort Wayne as a key step to statehood for
Indiana. Peaceful relations with Native Americans would
encourage white people to settle in the territory.

Harrison had not invited Tecumseh to take part in these negotiations. When Tecumseh learned of the treaty, he became enraged. The chiefs who signed the treaty had received gifts, but they were robbing future generations of their birthright. Angry warriors flocked to Prophetstown, anxious for a fight.

A FATEFUL MEETING

Although Harrison did not trust the Prophet, he invited him to negotiate a peace settlement to prevent bloodshed. Tecumseh informed Harrison that he would come instead. On the hot evening of Saturday, August 12, 1810, Tecumseh arrived in Vincennes, accompanied by about four hundred warriors, their faces painted for war.

Tecumseh and several members of his group visited Grouseland on Tuesday, August 15. Harrison greeted them on the porch. He and Tecumseh then walked alone to a shady grove. Tecumseh began by voicing his anger about the Treaty of Fort Wayne. The whites, he said, had already come too far onto Indian lands. The tribal leaders who had agreed to the treaty had no authority to sell land that did not belong to them, for the land belonged to all the Indians. During the next two days, Tecumseh and Harrison argued, but they kept talking. At one point, Tecumseh made an impassioned plea for his people:

> *Once there were no white men in all this country; then it belonged to red men, children of the same parents, placed on it by the Great Spirit, to keep it, to travel over it, to eat its fruits, and fill it with the same race—once a happy race, but now made*

Tecumseh (standing left) speaks with Harrison on the grounds of Grouseland.

———————— ✧

miserable by the white people, who are never contented, but always encroaching [trespassing].

Then, on the third day of discussions, Tecumseh lost his temper and called Harrison a liar. This outburst brought Harrison to his feet with his sword drawn. Several warriors lying nearby in the grass rushed to Tecumseh's side. Tecumseh, though angry, remained calm. He simply turned and left without another word.

Later that afternoon, Tecumseh sent word to Harrison that he was ready to resume talks. He asked Harrison to reconsider the Treaty of Fort Wayne and suggested that failure to do so would have serious consequences. Surely the whites had enough land already and did not need more. Harrison could not meet Tecumseh's demand. The United States had acquired the land legally, and the government would defend its rights by war if necessary. The next day, Tecumseh and his warriors left Vincennes.

TIPPECANOE

After the meeting with Tecumseh, Harrison believed that war with the Indians was inevitable. He wanted to strike first to disrupt Tecumseh's plans. But Congress, President James Madison, and the War Department hesitated. After many months of wrangling, the government at last agreed to let Harrison invade Indiana Territory and destroy Prophetstown. Bidding farewell to his wife; his new infant son, Carter Bassett; and his seven other children, Harrison set out.

President James Madison
———— ✧ ————

In October 1811, while Tecumseh was away from the village, Harrison left for Prophetstown. One regular army company, two militia companies, and a group of volunteers accompanied him. By November 6, the force was within one mile of the village. The Indians knew of Harrison's arrival, and a chief rode out to warn him that he was trespassing on Native American land. Harrison ignored the warning. He prepared to make camp.

At a council of war, the Indians decided to attack Harrison before he and his men struck the village. The Prophet held back. He said that he would not fight, but he would use all of his spiritual powers to aid the warriors.

In the hours before dawn on November 7, warriors crept through the cold drizzle. They hoped to find the soldiers asleep. The campfires that Harrison had allowed his men to keep burning all night lighted the way. Harrison

———————————— ✧ ————————————

Harrison (left, on horseback) and his men fight the Indians in the battle at Tippecanoe.

and his men were not prepared. Warriors ran out of the woods and charged into the camp. They believed that the Prophet's magic would shield them. Harrison ordered his soldiers to charge on horseback. The Indians left when they ran out of ammunition. Harrison and his men then advanced on the abandoned village.

Both sides suffered serious losses in the battle at Tippecanoe (so called because it took place along the banks of the Tippecanoe River). But the Indians lost more of their fighters. The battle also broke the Prophet's influence—his magic had failed. When Tecumseh returned in January 1812, he assumed sole command of the Indian alliance. For Harrison, the victory he claimed at Tippecanoe was bittersweet. While he had destroyed an empty Prophetstown, his decision to keep the campfires burning had perhaps cost lives. And Harrison had no doubt that Tecumseh would rally the Indians to continue the fight.

WAR OF 1812

The United States' trouble with Indians on the frontier paled in comparison to international tensions. On June 18, 1812, war broke out between the United States and Great Britain. The conflict centered on U.S. trading rights. For years the British had tried to keep the United States from trading with France, Great Britain's long-standing enemy. In addition to interfering with U.S. trade, British ships had begun stopping U.S. vessels on the high seas and forcing U.S. sailors to serve in the British Royal Navy. The U.S. government had protested but to no avail. President Madison had finally had enough. In June 1812, he asked Congress to declare war.

U.S. leaders also understood that the war against Great Britain was related to the struggle against the Indians. If the Americans could get the British out of North America, the Indians would no longer have an ally. Forced to go it alone, they might prove more manageable—or at least less eager for war.

In September 1812, President Madison made Harrison a general and put him in command of the army in the Northwest. Harrison had several assignments. He needed to protect U.S. settlements in the West from British and Indian attacks. He was also ordered to take back Detroit from the British, who had captured the city in July. Finally, Madison instructed Harrison to coordinate operations for an invasion of Canada. To concentrate fully on his military duties, the thirty-nine-year-old Harrison resigned the governorship of Indiana Territory in December 1812.

BATTLE OF THE THAMES

By early March 1813, Harrison had been promoted twice, first to major general and then to brigadier general. He also welcomed the birth of his ninth child, Anna Tuthill. During the months that followed, Harrison led his men in minor engagements against the British and the Native Americans. After Commander Oliver Hazard Perry captured the British fleet on Lake Erie in September 1813, he helped transfer Harrison's army across the lake. (Some historians question whether Harrison was with them.)

On October 5, 1813, Harrison and Perry led an army of thirty-five hundred troops against a combined force of seven hundred British soldiers and one thousand Indian warriors at Moraviantown, along the Thames River in

Oliver Hazard Perry (standing) defeated the British fleet on Lake Erie.
——————— ✧

Ontario, Canada. Colonel Henry Proctor commanded the British troops, while Tecumseh commanded the Indians.

At Moraviantown the U.S. Army won a total victory. The British soldiers fled or surrendered. The Indians fought fiercely, but they scattered after Tecumseh died on the battlefield. The day after the Battle of the Thames, U.S. soldiers searched the battlefield for Tecumseh's body. They never found it, leading many people to believe that the great warrior had escaped. The site of Tecumseh's grave remains unknown.

The Battle of the Thames was the most important land battle of the War of 1812 in the Northwest. Although the battle did not end the war against Great Britain, the victory broke up Tecumseh's Native American confederacy.

The Battle of the Thames (above, with Harrison on horseback)
was a key battle in the War of 1812 (1812–1815).

———————— ✧ ————————

Harrison's part in the victory at the Thames, as well as his distinguished record of service, should have earned him praise in Washington. But his accomplishments had the opposite effect. Secretary of War John Armstrong was so jealous of Harrison's success that he tried to interfere with Harrison's command. He issued contradictory orders and, in some cases, sent commands to Harrison's aides without informing Harrison himself. Armstrong's actions led one of Harrison's officers to write, "The people at Washington have got scared of Harrison's victories. They are afraid a few more might make him President. . . . You will not see them give Harrison another

command . . . they will simply leave him . . . where he
can gain no more victories."

Harrison resigned his
commission and left the
service, marking the end of
an extraordinary military
career. In 1814 the
Harrisons' tenth and last
child, James Findlay, was
born. In September 1815,
Harrison negotiated a
peace treaty with nine
Indian tribes. He then
journeyed home to his
family and, he hoped, a
quiet, private life.

John Armstrong

——— ◇ ———

*Many people who met Harrison (above) thought
he did not look like a general.*

CHAPTER SIX

THE ROAD TO
THE WHITE HOUSE

*Let Van [Buren] from his coolers
of silver drink wine
And lounge on his cushioned settee,
Our man on a buckeye bench can recline,
Content with hard cider is he.*
—campaign song supporting Harrison, 1840

By the spring of 1814, William Henry Harrison had
retired to the farm he had bought in North Bend, Ohio,
years earlier when he was still a young army officer. The
area held special memories as the place where he met
and later married his wife, Anna. Harrison was forty-one
years old. An acquaintance described him as "small and
rather [pale]-looking . . . [he] does not exactly meet the
associations that connect themselves with the name of
general. . . . But he grows upon the eye. . . . His eye is

brilliant and there is a great deal of ardour and vivacity in his manner."

Although Harrison had earned an annual salary of $2,400 ($23,500) as an army general, he was struggling financially. Unlike many people who had made fortunes buying land in the West, Harrison was deeply in debt. With no job prospects in sight, he turned to farming.

THE LOG CABIN

The Harrison family's new home was a far cry from the governor's mansion at Grouseland. Located in the town of North Bend, the house was little more than a log cabin. The farm was large, though, with more than three thousand acres of land, as well as many orchards and gardens.

Harrison remodeled his small log cabin in North Bend into a large house suitable for entertaining (above).

Soon Harrison was at work remodeling the tiny house. He added two large wings on either side. In time, the small, four-room home grew into a house of sixteen rooms. Harrison kept no slaves, but he had servants to help with the everyday chores.

As at Grouseland, Harrison opened his home to guests and relatives. Stories of his hospitality were legendary. So many visitors came that in a single year, they ate more than 365 hams. Despite the cost of entertaining so many people, Harrison kept his doors open. One visitor wrote that "his house was open to all the neighbors, who entered without ceremony and [assumed] a footing of entire equality."

CONGRESSMAN HARRISON

In 1816 Harrison decided to run for the U.S. Congress. Even though he lived in a small town, he still kept in touch with influential politicians. Harrison easily won the election against four other candidates for a seat in the U.S. House of Representatives.

As a congressional representative, Harrison served on the Committee on Public Lands and was chairman of the Committee on Militia. He took an active part in debates and became a familiar figure on the floor of the House. He offered a bill that required military training for all young men. The bill failed to become law, but another of Harrison's legislative efforts passed—a bill to provide funds for disabled veterans and the widows and children of soldiers killed in war. Despite his political successes, Harrison was still burdened by financial problems. In 1819 he returned home to North Bend. "Our debts are extremely large and very pressing," he wrote to a friend. His farm was making little money, and Harrison had made some bad business deals. To prevent himself from sinking further into debt, he sadly sold off some of his farmland.

RETURN TO WASHINGTON

Harrison did not stay at North Bend long. Late in 1819, he won a seat in the Ohio Senate, where he served one term. In 1822 he again ran for a seat in the U.S. House of Representatives. He lost a hard-fought and bitter campaign, but he decided to try his luck again in 1825. This time he won election to the U.S Senate.

Harrison joined the Senate in March 1825. One observer noted that Harrison entered the Senate chambers wearing a long black coat, a wool hat, and cowhide boots. Harrison chaired the military and militia committees and worked hard to support President John Quincy Adams. Harrison hoped to become Adams's running mate in the election of 1828. Much to Harrison's disappointment, however, Adams decided on someone else. Yet Harrison continued to support Adams's programs. Like Adams, Harrison became a strong advocate for an active federal government that promoted business interests and economic expansion.

A SHORT STAY

Although he did not select Harrison as his running mate, Adams was grateful for Harrison's loyalty. In the spring of 1828, Adams appointed Harrison the first U.S. minister to Colombia. (The South American country had won independence from Spain several years earlier.) Harrison got the job in part because his friend Henry Clay, a powerful senator from Kentucky, had pushed for his nomination.

Clay had mixed motives. He wanted to help his friend. But he also wanted to prevent Harrison from becoming Adams's running mate. If Adams won the election, his vice president would stand a good chance of later becoming president—an office that Clay wanted for himself. In the end, Clay's scheming came to nothing. Adams lost the election of 1828 to his political rival, Andrew Jackson, a Democrat from Tennessee.

Harrison's first position in a foreign country ended abruptly. Not long after he arrived in Colombia in early 1829, Harrison suggested that President Simón Bolívar should take care not to become a dictator. Bolívar, who had fought to free much of South America from Spanish rule, took offense. Jackson replaced Harrison a month later.

Latin American revolutionary leader Simón Bolívar freed Colombia and many other South American countries from Spanish rule in the early 1800s.

HARD TIMES

By the end of 1829, Harrison was back home at North Bend. His homecoming was not entirely happy. His financial situation had worsened. Not only did Harrison himself owe more than $20,000 (about $370,000), but two of his sons had also gotten into debt. To pay off what he and his sons owed, Harrison sold more land. Harrison also had the added burden of supporting the children of his son William Henry Harrison Jr., who died at the age of thirty-five.

In 1830 Harrison found work as a clerk of courts in Cincinnati. The job was a far cry from his important positions as territorial governor, army general, congressman, and senator, but he was grateful for the income. About this time, a French traveler visiting Cincinnati caught a glimpse of Harrison. The Frenchman noted:

> I had observed at the hotel table a man of about medium height, stout and muscular, and of about the age of sixty years yet with the active step and lively air of youth. I had been struck with his open and cheerful expression . . . and a certain air of command[,] which appeared through his plain dress. "That," said my friend, "is General Harrison, clerk of the Cincinnati court. . . . He is now poor, with a numerous family, neglected by the federal government, although yet vigorous, because he has the independence to think for himself."

RISING FORTUNES

Harrison remained in political retirement for four years. His luck improved in 1834. By that time, the political landscape had changed considerably. During the 1820s, the only citizens eligible to vote were wealthy white men—those who owned property. By the 1830s, states had begun to abandon these so-called property qualifications and the number of white men who could vote rose dramatically. (Women, blacks, and Native Americans remained ineligible.) To appeal to these voters, political parties adopted new strategies.

At the same time, the political parties themselves were changing. After 1820 the old Federalist Party had disappeared, and a new party had begun to form. Formally organized in 1834, the Whig Party was a loose organization united in opposition to Andrew Jackson. The Whigs—under the leadership of senators Henry Clay and Daniel Webster and newspaper publisher Horace Greeley—supported a strong federal government. They favored reorganizing the national bank and building more roads, bridges, and canals. They also supported a tariff (a tax on imports). Tariffs raise the price of goods made overseas. The Whigs hoped that if foreign goods cost more, people would buy products made in the United States instead.

By 1836 the Whig Party was gaining momentum. But the Whigs needed a candidate to challenge the Democrats in the coming presidential election. Democrat Andrew Jackson had won the elections of 1828 and 1832 largely on the strength of his military record. Jackson had earned a national reputation for fighting Indians and for defeating the British in the battle at New Orleans during the War of 1812.

In 1836 the Whigs decided to nominate more than one Whig candidate, including Harrison, to challenge the Democratic presidential nominee, Martin Van Buren of New York. With so many candidates in the race, the Whigs hoped that none would receive the necessary majority. If that happened, the election would be decided in the House of Representatives. The representatives would cast votes to choose the next president. However, the Whigs' strategy failed. Van Buren won the election. Harrison received the most votes of all the Whig contenders, winning seventy-three electoral votes.

Soon after Van Buren's inauguration in 1837, Whig Party officials began working to secure Harrison's nomination for the election of 1840. Harrison could hardly believe this change of fortune. He wrote to a friend, "I have news still more strange to tell you. . . . Some folks are silly enough to have formed a plan to make a President of the United States out of this clerk and clodhopper."

AN EARLY START

Not long after Van Buren took office, the United States suffered a depression (economic downturn), known as the Panic of 1837. Production and sales of U.S. goods fell. Businesses failed and people lost their jobs. Van Buren's inability to revive the economy hurt his chances for reelection. Taking advantage of Van Buren's misfortunes, Harrison took the unusual step of campaigning in person. In the past, candidates had stayed home and allowed supporters to speak for them. Americans considered it improper for a candidate to seem too eager to win office. Harrison ignored the old rules of political campaigning. Instead, he traveled throughout the country to gather support for his nomination as a Whig candidate for the presidency.

At the Whigs' nominating convention in December 1839, delegates bypassed Henry Clay. The Whigs feared that Clay had made too many political enemies. Instead,

John Tyler was Harrison's running mate in the 1840 election.
——————— ✧

the delegates chose Harrison. Their choice for the vice-presidential nominee was John Tyler, an anti-Jackson Democrat, who, like Harrison, hailed from Charles City County, Virginia.

Although Harrison was nearly sixty-seven years old, he appeared energetic and healthy. In addition, his military reputation rivaled that of Andrew Jackson. Rumor even had it that Harrison had single-handedly killed Tecumseh at the Battle of the Thames.

A NEW KIND OF CAMPAIGN

On the morning of June 6, 1840, on the steps of the National Hotel in Columbus, Ohio, William Henry Harrison became the first presidential candidate ever to make a campaign speech on his own behalf. A reporter for the *Cleveland Adviser* strongly disapproved, writing: "When was there ever before such a spectacle as a candidate for the Presidency, traversing the country advocating his own claims for that high and responsible station? . . . Never! . . . the precedent thus set by Harrison appears to us a bad one." For good or ill, Harrison had launched the modern political

Harrison's campaign posters focused on his career in Indiana Territory.

✧ ————————————

campaign. Afterward, all presidential candidates actively campaigned for themselves.

Harrison traveled the country and made speeches. But as he stumped (campaigned), he avoided taking a stand on the issues of the day. Instead, he focused on personality and character traits that set him apart from his opponent, President Van Buren. Harrison portrayed himself as a man of the people—a simple, hardworking western farmer who lived in a log cabin. Van Buren, by contrast, was an eastern aristocrat who indulged in luxury.

The idea for this comparison came from Nicholas Biddle, a Philadelphia banker. Biddle advised one of Harrison's campaign managers to "let [Harrison] rely entirely on the past, not the future. Let him say not one single word about his principles, or his creed—let him say nothing—promise nothing. Let no committee, no convention, no town meeting ever extract from him a single word about what he thinks now, or what he will do hereafter." The Whigs hoped that by not taking a stand, Harrison would offend no one.

"TIPPECANOE AND TYLER, TOO!"

Harrison's campaign was the best organized and most exciting one Americans had ever seen. To attract voters, the Whigs held parades, picnics, and rallies in towns and cities across the nation. Participants enjoyed music, food, whiskey, and hot-air balloon rides. Barbecue smoke and banners filled

———————————— ✧ ————————————

*Harrison's supporters hold a parade in front
of Whig headquarters in Philadelphia.*

The expression "keep the ball rolling," as printed on this campaign poster, started in the Harrison-Tyler presidential campaign of 1840.

———— ✧

the air. At one picnic in Wheeling, Virginia, the crowd devoured 360 hams, 26 sheep, 20 calves, 1,500 pounds of beef, 8,000 pounds of bread, 1,000 pounds of cheese, and 4,500 pies.

In Cleveland a group of Whigs created a huge tin ball, twelve feet across, that they pushed all the way to the Ohio state capital of Columbus. There they met up with other Whigs who had an even bigger ball, made of cowhide and pulled by twenty-four white oxen. Harrison's motto, "Keep the ball rolling," suggested that he would "roll over" the Democrats in November.

Campaign songs and slogans celebrated Harrison's life on the frontier and his victory at Tippecanoe. Harrison's nickname was Old Tip, a reference to the battle. People also showed their support for Harrison by posting hand-crafted signs along rivers and in lumberyards. Pundits (political commentators) called these early forms of political advertising Harrison Wood, Whig Wood, or Tippecanoe Wood.

SOUVENIRS

Harrison's presidential campaign marked the beginning of the large-scale manufacture of political souvenirs. Harrison supporters could buy neckties showing Harrison and Tyler, a handkerchief with a U.S. flag and Harrison's face on it, or Tippecanoe Shaving Soap. Among the most popular items were miniature log cabin whiskey decanters (glass bottles), which campaign workers gave to travelers and boat workers on the Erie Canal.

——————✧
Harrison's image could even be found on cream pitchers like this one.

Campaign songs were
printed with covers
illustrating Harrison's
rural western life.

✧ ────────────

To fight back, the Democrats characterized Harrison as
a country bumpkin. "Harrison for President!" proclaimed
one Democratic campaign pamphlet. "Why he's just a
backwoodsman. He eats corn pone [corn bread] and drinks
cider. His mother still lives in a log cabin." But the criti-
cism backfired. Harrison's campaign managers used similar
descriptions to portray Harrison as a man of the people. At
one Whig rally, a speaker exclaimed:

> Log cabins sirs, were the dwelling places of the
> founders of our Republic! It was a log cabin that
> sheltered the daring pioneers of liberty. . . . It

was in view of the rock of Plymouth, my friends,
that the Puritans of New England first erected
the log cabins which sheltered the mothers and
fathers of a race which now [covers] a continent.
In response, the crowd yelled, "Tippecanoe and
Tyler, too!" The slogan was one of the most
memorable sayings of the campaign.

Soon the image of a log cabin began appearing on everything from caps to banners and buttons. To show support for their candidate, the Whigs rolled out large barrels of hard cider (an alcoholic beverage made from apples) decorated with log cabins. The Whigs raised, or built, cabins in Harrison's honor throughout the country. Even in Van Buren's home state of New York, a large log cabin went up on Broadway near Prince Street in New York City. Whenever a cabin was built, people celebrated with a parade, a feast, and a lot of drinking.

Although Harrison came from an upper-class family and had a college education, the campaign identified him as a rustic frontiersman. Americans were so taken by the "log cabin and hard cider campaign" that they did not notice that Harrison had said nothing about his political views. In his speeches, Harrison merely pledged to work with Congress and to listen to the people's wishes.

Harrison was nearly sixty-eight years old when he won the 1840 presidential election.

CHAPTER SEVEN

THE SHORTEST PRESIDENCY

*Sir, I wish you to understand the true
principles of the government. I wish them
carried out. I ask nothing more.*
—William Henry Harrison's last words, April 4, 1841

Even without taking a strong stand on major issues of the day, Harrison had broad appeal across the country. He drew support from settlers in the West, bankers in the Northeast, and planters in the South. When Americans voted in November 1840, turnout was staggering. Approximately 2.4 million people cast ballots, a 50 percent increase over the 1836 election. Harrison won in nineteen of the twenty-six states, including Van Buren's home state of New York. The popular vote was close—Harrison won by fewer than 150,000 votes. In the electoral college, however, Harrison's 234 votes to Van Buren's 60 gave him a spectacular victory.

While Harrison was elated, his wife was more reserved. "I wish that my husband's friends had left him where he is," she said, "happy and contented in retirement." But Anna resolved to support her husband as he prepared to become president of the United States. Harrison's first official act as president-elect was to resign as clerk of the Cincinnati court.

PREPARING TO TAKE OFFICE

January 26, 1841, dawned clear and cold. Harrison stood before a cheering crowd on the steamboat *Ben Franklin*, docked at the Cincinnati riverfront. Earlier, as he had made his way to the docks, a jubilant crowd had followed. Some were on foot, others in wagons or on horseback. All were coming to wish the new president a safe journey. Mrs. Harrison was not on the boat with her husband. She was at home sick and planned to follow him to Washington later in the spring.

Before setting out, Harrison made a brief, somber speech. "Gentlemen and fellow-citizens," he began, "perhaps this is the last time I may have the pleasure of speaking to you on earth or seeing you. I bid you farewell, if forever, fare thee well."

As cannons boomed across the river, Harrison's boat began the journey to Baltimore. A military band on board played, and a militia onshore fired a salute. People gathered along the route to cheer Harrison. Even at night, bonfires lighted the shores in honor of Old Tip. Stopping in Hagerstown, Maryland, on his way to Washington, Harrison enjoyed a warm welcome from both Whigs and Democrats. As part of the ceremony, Harrison received a 112-pound cake decorated with his campaign slogans.

On February 5, Harrison's boat landed at Frederick, Maryland. From there, Harrison traveled by train to

Washington. Everywhere he stopped, people waited to shake his hand. On February 9, 1841—Harrison's sixty-eighth birthday—he rode into Washington on his favorite horse, Old Whitey. After meeting with Whig and Democratic leaders, Harrison spoke with other city officials. It seemed that everyone was looking for a political appointment of some kind. Loyal members of the Whig Party overwhelmed Harrison with requests for patronage (the practice of awarding government positions to people who had supported a candidate and campaigned on his behalf).

Harrison next called at the White House to meet with the outgoing president, Martin Van Buren. The two exchanged polite greetings and spoke about issues facing the nation. Van Buren liked Harrison but thought he was unprepared for the burdens of office. Another observer also noted Harrison's carefree manner:

> *Passing through the crowd on Pennsylvania Avenue was . . . an elderly gentleman dressed in black, and not remarkably well dressed, with a . . . military air, but stooping a little, bowing to one, shaking hands with another, and cracking a joke with the third. And this man was William Henry Harrison, the President-elect of this great empire . . . and there he went unattended and unconscious of the dignity of his position—the* man *among men.*

MR. PRESIDENT

On March 4, Harrison took the oath of office on the East Portico of the Capitol. Afterward, he gave his first speech as president. Despite the cold, damp weather, Harrison refused to wear a hat, overcoat, or gloves. In his speech, the new president promised to maintain a clear separation of powers between the judicial, legislative, and executive branches of the government. That way, no branch would become dominant. He also criticized the spoils system. The spoils system gave important government jobs as rewards to the president's supporters, even though they might not be suitable for the jobs. At another point in his speech, Harrison

Despite the bad weather, Harrison's inauguration at the Capitol drew a large, lively crowd.

A page from Harrison's inaugural address given on March 4, 1841

——————— ✧

attacked the abolitionist movement, stating that it had weakened the bonds of the Union.

Harrison's inaugural speech is still the longest on record. It contained more than eight thousand words and took more than an hour and forty minutes to deliver.

Soon after taking office, Harrison fell ill with a cold, but he busied himself with the task of governing the nation. A week into his administration, tensions with Great Britain raised the prospect of war, but skillful diplomacy resolved the crisis. Harrison also called a special session of Congress to consider the Whig legislative agenda, which included discussions about raising tariffs and establishing a third national bank.

Harrison still constantly faced a barrage of office seekers. They lingered in the White House halls, waiting to see him. Harrison's coat pockets bulged with papers on which men had written their requests for a government job. In exasperation, Harrison exclaimed, "These applications, will they never cease?"

A TRAGIC END

One morning in late March, Harrison went out shopping at the Washington meat and fish markets for food for the White House. As usual, he didn't wear a hat or overcoat. While out, he was caught in a heavy rainstorm. A few days later, the cold that he had been nursing for weeks suddenly grew worse. Harrison's doctors confined him to bed, but

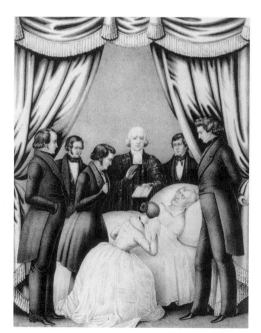

✧ ————————————

Harrison lies in his bed surrounded by a doctor, his niece and nephew, and members of his cabinet.

they assured him he was not in any danger. Harrison believed otherwise, telling his nurse, "I am ill, very ill, much more so than they think me."

On April 3, Harrison began drifting in and out of consciousness. In the early hours of Sunday, April 4, 1841, William Henry Harrison died of pneumonia. He had been president for just one month.

News of Harrison's death stunned the nation. It was the first time in the history of the United States that a president had died in office. Anna Harrison, who had been preparing to join her husband in Washington, arrived in time to attend his funeral.

At his home in Virginia, Tyler (right) receives the news of Harrison's death. As the first person to be vice president when a president died, Tyler was under a lot of pressure to keep the government going.

On April 7, cannon fire thundered in the morning gloom, signaling the start of Harrison's funeral procession. Harrison's body lay in the East Room of the White House. His coffin was shrouded in black, with a glass lid that showed his face. More than twenty clergy gathered around the coffin. Nearly all the political leaders in Washington paid their final respects. Outside, thousands of mourners stood at the White House gates, while others gathered along the route to the Capitol, where Harrison's body would lay in state.

At half past eleven, the funeral service began. A priest from Saint John's Episcopal Church spoke of Harrison's great faith, his recent purchase of a new Bible, and his service to God and country. After the funeral, twenty-four pallbearers wearing white sashes carried out the coffin. Fourteen volunteer military companies assembled along Pennsylvania Avenue. As the funeral procession carried the body to the Capitol, more than ten thousand people lined the streets to say farewell. Harrison's horse, Old Whitey, marched in the procession without a rider.

Months later, Harrison's widow shipped his remains back to North Bend. Harrison's tomb faces west, overlooking the Ohio River—the same river that carried Harrison on his journey to the frontier as a young man.

LEGACY

William Henry Harrison was president for too short a time to have left a political legacy. It is difficult to know how his presidency would have gone had he lived, though historians have made some guesses. Harrison likely would have remained engaged in settling the West and negotiating

SOME PRESIDENTIAL FIRSTS

William Henry Harrison, who took office at the age of sixty-eight, was the oldest man elected president until sixty-nine-year-old Ronald Reagan won the election in 1980. Harrison was the first president to die in office and had the shortest term of office. In addition, Harrison was the only president to have a grandson elected to the presidency (Benjamin Harrison). William Henry Harrison was the president with the most children from one marriage: ten. Not surprisingly, he was also the president with the most grandchildren (48) and great-grandchildren (106).

Benjamin Harrison was the only grandson of a president to be elected president.

treaties with Native Americans. He would have had to grapple with the issue of slavery and its expansion into new territories. Harrison was also very concerned with political reform. He wanted to get rid of corruption.

Harrison has not disappeared from the history books, however. Historians remember his military service and the role he played in western settlement as a territorial governor.

Harrison's tomb (above) *is in North Bend, Ohio.*

———— ✧ ————

Harrison's chief political legacy is as a presidential candidate. He changed the nature of political campaigns, ushering in modern campaign tactics. The son of a Virginia aristocrat, Harrison believed in the common man's ability to contribute to the American experiment in self-government. And until his untimely death, Harrison worked hard to ensure that the promise of a government for and by the people would remain constant and true.

TIMELINE

1773 William Henry Harrison is born February 9 in Charles City County, Virginia.

1774 William's father, Benjamin Harrison V, becomes a delegate to the Continental Congress, and the family moves to Philadelphia.

1775 The American Revolution begins.

1781 British and Hessian troops attack Berkeley, the Harrison family plantation.

1783 The American Revolution ends when the British sign the Treaty of Paris to recognize U.S. independence.

1784 The Harrison family returns to their home at Berkeley.

1787 Harrison enters Hampden-Sidney College in Virginia.

1790 Harrison begins studies with Dr. Andrew Leiper in Richmond, Virginia.

1791 Harrison enrolls in the Medical School of Pennsylvania. In August he enlists in the army.

1793 Harrison serves as aide-de-camp under General Anthony Wayne.

1794 Harrison fights in the battle at Fallen Timbers against the Shawnee, Miami, and other Indians.

1795 On August 3, U.S. and tribal leaders sign the Treaty of Greenville, which gives the United States a large area of land in the Ohio Valley. Shawnee leader Tecumseh rejects the treaty and works to unite the tribes against white settlement. On November 25, Harrison marries Anna Symmes.

1797 Harrison receives a promotion to captain and takes command of Fort Washington.

1798 Harrison resigns from the army and is appointed secretary of the Northwest Territory.

1799 Harrison is elected as a delegate to the U.S. House of Representatives from the Northwest Territory.

1800 The Harrison Land Act passes in Congress, making it easier for people to buy land in the Northwest Territory. Harrison is appointed governor of the newly created Indiana Territory.

1801 Construction begins on Grouseland, Harrison's home in Vincennes, Indiana.

1802 President Thomas Jefferson grants Harrison the power to make treaties with Native Americans.

1803 Harrison proposes a law to allow slavery in Indiana Territory, but antislavery groups fight the measure.

1806 War looms as tensions rise between white settlers and Native Americans in Indiana Territory. Shawnee spiritual leader Tenskwatawa, known as the Prophet, wins supporters by successfully predicting an eclipse of the sun.

1808 Tecumseh and the Prophet establish an encampment known as Prophetstown at the junction of the Tippecanoe and Wabash rivers. Through the Treaty of Fort Wayne, Harrison buys millions of acres in Indiana Territory from several tribes. Tecumseh is enraged.

1809 Congress passes a law banning slavery in Indiana Territory, a political defeat for Harrison.

1810 Harrison and Tecumseh meet in August to negotiate peace, but the talks end with no agreement.

1811 Harrison and U.S. soldiers fight the Shawnee in the battle at Tippecanoe.

1812 Harrison resigns as governor to take a commission as a major general of the Kentucky militia during the War of 1812. He later is commissioned a general of the U.S. Army of the Northwest.

1813	U.S. troops defeat the British at the Battle of the Thames in Ontario, Canada.
1814	Harrison resigns from the army and returns home to farm in North Bend, Ohio.
1816	Harrison is elected to the U.S. House of Representatives from Ohio.
1819–1821	Harrison serves as a member of the Ohio Senate.
1822	Harrison runs unsuccessfully for a seat in the U.S. House of Representatives.
1825	Harrison is elected to the U.S. Senate to represent Ohio.
1828	Harrison is appointed the first diplomatic envoy to Colombia, South America.
1829	Harrison retires to his farm at North Bend.
1829–1836	Harrison works as clerk of the county court in Cincinnati.
1836	Harrison makes an unsuccessful run for the presidency as a candidate for the Whig Party.
1837	The Panic of 1837 crushes the U.S. economy, causing many business failures and widespread unemployment.
1839	Harrison wins the Whig Party nomination for president.
1840	Harrison becomes the first presidential candidate to make speeches on his own behalf. He wins the presidential election with more than 52 percent of the popular vote, defeating incumbent president Martin Van Buren.
1841	Harrison is inaugurated on March 4. Less than a month later, he becomes seriously ill and dies on April 4 at the White House.

SOURCE NOTES

7. "William Henry Harrison Quotes," *ThinkExist.com Quotations*, 2006, http://en.thinkexist.com/quotes/william_henry_harrison/ (July 20, 2006).

10. James Albert Green, *William Henry Harrison: His Life and Times* (Richmond, VA: Garrett and Massie, 1941), 1.

23. Freeman Cleaves, *Old Tippecanoe: William Henry Harrison and His Time* (New York: Charles Scribner's Sons, 1939), 7.

24. Ibid., 12.

29. "Tecumseh," *National Park Service*, n.d., http://www.nps.gov/pevi/HTML/Tecumseh.html (February 1, 2006).

37. Cleaves, *Old Tippecanoe,* 21.

39. Charles Stewart Todd and Benjamin Drake, *Sketches of the Military Services of William Henry Harrison* (New York: Arno Press, 1975), 21.

40. Cleaves, *Old Tippecanoe*, 23.

42. Ibid., 25.

42. Dorothy Burne Goebel and Julius Goebel Jr., *Generals in the White House* (New York: Doubleday, Doran and Company, 1945), 101.

43. Cleaves, *Old Tippecanoe*, 26.

49. Dorothy Burne Goebel, *William Henry Harrison: A Political Biography* (Indianapolis: Historical Bureau of the Indiana Library and Historical Department, 1926), 51–52.

52. Cleaves, *Old Tippecanoe*, 36.

52. Goebel, *William Henry Harrison*, 58.

54. Cleaves, *Old Tippecanoe*, 34.

59. Green, *William Henry Harrison: His Life and Times*, 129.

63. Goebel, *William Henry Harrison*, 112.

63. Cleaves, *Old Tippecanoe*, 55.

63. Ibid., 54.

65–66. Reed Beard, "The Battle of Tippecanoe," August 1, 1889, *RootsWeb*, http://www.rootsweb.com/~usgenweb/ky/tippecanoe/chapter3.html (February 1, 2006).

72–73. Cleaves, *Old Tippecanoe*, 214.

75. David E. Johnson, "1840 Presidential Campaign: A Ceaseless Torrent of Music," *The HistoryNet.com*, 2005, http://www.historynet.com/ah/bltorrectofmusic/ (February 5, 2006).

75–76. Cleaves, *Old Tippecanoe*, 230.

77. Goebel, *William Henry Harrison*, 205.

77. Cleaves, *Old Tippecanoe*, 247.

80. Ibid., 291.

82. Ibid., 292–93.

83. Nicholas Van Hoffman, "Campaign Craziness: A Cracker-Barrel History," *New Republic*, November 5, 1984, 17.

84–85. Ibid.

87. Janet Podell and Steven Anzovin, *Facts about the Presidents: A Compilation of Biographical and Historical Information* (New York: H. W. Wilson, 2001), 78.

88. Ibid.

88–89. Ibid.

89. Ibid.

91. Goebel and Goebel, *Generals in the White House*, 117.

91–92. Cleaves, *Old Tippecanoe*, 328.

92. Ibid., 331.

93. Ibid., 335.

96. William A. Degregorio, *The Complete Book of U.S. Presidents* (New York: Wings Books, 1993), 145.

97. Ibid., 145.

SELECTED BIBLIOGRAPHY

Adams, Charles Francis, ed. *Works of John Adams: Second President of the United States: With a Life of the Author, Notes and Illustrations.* Vol. 2. Boston: Charles C. Little and James Brown, 1850.

Cleaves, Freeman. *Old Tippecanoe: William Henry Harrison and His Time.* New York: Charles Scribner's Sons, 1939.

Cronin, John William, and W. Harvey Wise Jr. *A Bibliography of William Henry Harrison, John Tyler, James Knox Polk.* Washington, D.C.: Riverford Publishing Co., 1935.

Degregorio, William A. *The Complete Book of U.S. Presidents.* New York: Wings Books, 1993.

Durfee, David A., comp. *William Henry Harrison, 1773–1841: John Tyler, 1790–1862: Chronology, Documents, Bibliographical Aids.* Dobbs Ferry, NY: Oceana Publications, 1970.

Esarey, Logan, ed. *Messages and Letters of William Henry Harrison.* 2 vols. 1922. Reprint. New York: Arno Press, 1975.

Goebel, Dorothy Burne. *William Henry Harrison: A Political Biography.* Indianapolis: Historical Bureau of the Indiana Library and Historical Department, 1926.

Goebel, Dorothy Burne, and Julius Goebel Jr. *Generals in the White House.* New York: Doubleday, Doran and Co., 1945.

Green, James Albert. *William Henry Harrison: His Life and Times.* Richmond, VA: Garrett & Massie, 1941.

Gunderson, Robert Gray. *The Log Cabin Campaign.* Westport, CT: Greenwood Press, 1957.

Horsman, Reginald. "William Henry Harrison: Virginia Gentleman in the Old Northwest." *Indiana Magazine of History,* (June 2000), 125–50.

Kane, Joseph Nathan, Janet Podell, and Steven Anzovin. *Facts About the Presidents: A Compilation of Biographical and Historical Information.* New York: H. W. Wilson, 2001.

Montgomery, Henry. *The Life of Major-General William H. Harrison, Ninth President of the United States*. Philadelphia: Porter & Coates, 1852.

Peterson, Norma Lois. *The Presidencies of William Henry Harrison & John Tyler*. Lawrence: University Press of Kansas, 1989.

Van Hoffman, Nicholas. "Campaign Craziness: A Cracker-Barrel History." *New Republic*, November 5, 1984.

Wills, Garry. *James Madison*. New York: Henry Holt and Company, 2002.

FURTHER READING AND WEBSITES

Aller, Susan Bivin, *Tecumseh*. Minneapolis: Lerner Publications Company, 2004.

The American Presidency
http://ap.grolier.com/article?assetid=0132910-0&templatename=/article/article.htmlbrowse?type=profiles
From Grolier Online, this encyclopedia article about Harrison and his life includes a link to Harrison's inaugural address.

American Presidents: Life Portraits
http://www.americanpresidents.org/presidents/president.asp?PresidentNumber=9
This site provides a brief overview of Harrison's life and presidency, with links and a bibliography.

Behrman, Carol. *The Indian Wars*. Minneapolis: Twenty-First Century Books, 2005.

Bohannon, Lisa Frederiksen. *The American Revolution*. Minneapolis: Twenty-First Century Books, 2004.

Childress, Diana. *The War of 1812*. Minneapolis: Twenty-First Century Books, 2004.

Evensen, Caroline Lazo. *Martin Van Buren*. Minneapolis: Twenty-First Century Books, 2005.

Gaines, Ann Graham. *William Henry Harrison: Our Ninth President*. New York: Child's World, 2001.

Havelin, Kate. *John Tyler*. Minneapolis: Twenty-First Century Books, 2005.

Indiana Governor William Henry Harrison
http://www.statelib.lib.in.us/www/ihb/govportraits/harrison.html
From the Indiana Historical Bureau, this overview of Harrison's life emphasizes his term as governor of the Indiana Territory.

Lillard, David. *William Henry Harrison*. New York: Enslow Books, 2003.

Ohio History Central: William Henry Harrison
http://www.ohiohistorycentral.org/ohc/history/h_indian/people/
harriswh.shtmlentry.php?rec=190
This biography of Harrison has links to other sites about Harrison.

Otfinoski, Steven. *William Henry Harrison: America's 9th President.*
Danbury, CT: Children's Press, 2003.

Peckham, Howard S. *William Henry Harrison: Young Tippecanoe.* New
York: Patria Press, 2001.

The White House—Presidential Biographies
http://www.whitehouse.gov/history/presidents/wh9.html
The White House website provides biographies of all the
presidents, including William Henry Harrison.

INDEX

About the Author

Meg Greene is a descendant of William Henry Harrison. She is a writer and historian living in Virginia.

⬧
